Space-ology

Living on
MARS

by Ellen Lawrence

Consultant:
Josh Barker
Space Communications Team
National Space Centre
Leicester, United Kingdom

BEARPORT PUBLISHING

New York, New York

Credits

Cover, © e7llena/Shutterstock; 4, © e7llena/Shutterstock; 5, © NASA/Public Domain and © Fotokostic/Shutterstock; 6, © Public Domain; 7T, © Ruby Tuesday Books; 7, © NASA; 8, © NASA; 9TL, © ESA; 9BL, © European Space Agency/Science Photo Library; 9R, © ESA/IBMP; 10, © Herschel Hoffmeyer/Shutterstock; 11, © e7llena/Shutterstock; 12T, © NASA; 12B, © Jan Kaliciak/Shutterstock; 13TR, © Fedorov Oleksiy/Shutterstock; 13, © Jan Kaliciak/Shutterstock; 14, © Photononstop/Superstock; 15, © NASA/Public Domain; 16, © NASA; 17, © NASA/Public Domain; 18, © NASA; 19TL, © NASA; 19, © Stocktrek Images Inc/Alamy; 20, © NASA; 21, © Dotted Yeti/Shutterstock; 22L, © RTImages/Shutterstock; 22R, © u3D/Shutterstock; 23TL, © e7llena/Shutterstock; 23TC, © NASA; 23TR, © e7llena/Shutterstock; 23BL, © Sergey Novikov/Shutterstock; 23BC, © Steve Lee (University of Colorado), Jim Bell (Cornell University), Mike Wolff (Space Science Institute), and NASA; 23BR, © Jaromir Chalabala/Shutterstock.

Publisher: Kenn Goin
Senior Editor: Joyce Tavolacci
Creative Director: Spencer Brinker
Photo Researcher: Ruth Owen Books

Library of Congress Cataloging-in-Publication Data

Names: Lawrence, Ellen, 1967– author.
Title: Living on Mars / by Ellen Lawrence.
Description: New York, New York : Bearport Publishing, [2019] | Series:
   Space-ology | Includes bibliographical references
   and index.
Identifiers: LCCN 2018053301 (print) | LCCN 2018054171 (ebook) | ISBN
   9781642802467 (ebook) | ISBN 9781642801774 (library)
Subjects: LCSH: Space colonies—Juvenile literature. | Space
   environment—Juvenile literature. | Space flight to Mars—Juvenile
   literature. | Planets—Environmental engineering—Juvenile literature. |
   Mars (Planet)—Exploration—Juvenile literature.
Classification: LCC TL795.7 (ebook) | LCC TL795.7 .L39 2019 (print) | DDC
   629.45/53—dc23
LC record available at https://lccn.loc.gov/2018053301

For more information, write to Bearport Publishing Company, Inc., 45 West 21st Street, Suite 3B, New York, New York 10010. Printed in the United States of America.

10 9 8 7 6 5 4 3

Contents

A Dangerous World

A man prepares to leave his home to pick up some food.

He puts on a special suit, gloves, and helmet. Why?

Without this protection, he will die.

He slowly walks from his small **habitat** to a giant greenhouse.

The man is a Marsonaut— one of the first humans to live on Mars!

Will humans one day live on Mars? Many scientists think so. The first step will be for astronauts to visit Mars. This could happen in the next ten years!

Welcome to Mars!

Mars is one of the closest planets to Earth, but it's a very different world.

It's dusty and rocky with no rivers, lakes, or oceans.

The only water is solid ice that's deep underground and at the planet's **poles**.

Sometimes, powerful windstorms cover Mars with dust.

How could humans possibly survive in this extreme place?

Earth

Mars

Mars is much smaller than Earth.

What things do you think humans will need to live on Mars? In a notebook, write a list of your ideas.

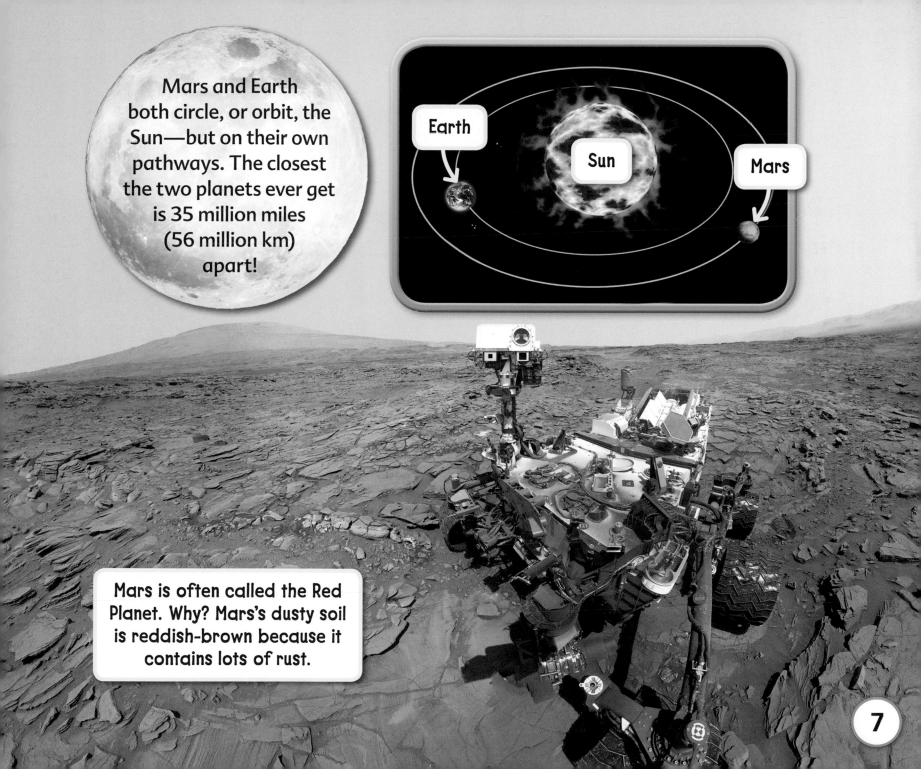

Mars and Earth both circle, or orbit, the Sun—but on their own pathways. The closest the two planets ever get is 35 million miles (56 million km) apart!

Earth

Sun

Mars

Mars is often called the Red Planet. Why? Mars's dusty soil is reddish-brown because it contains lots of rust.

A Long Journey

The journey to Mars will be very long and difficult.

It would take astronauts around nine months to fly from Earth to Mars.

In 2010, the Mars500 mission tested how a journey to Mars might affect humans.

Six men spent many months shut in a spacecraft-like machine on Earth.

Scientists studied the effects of the mission on the mens' minds and bodies.

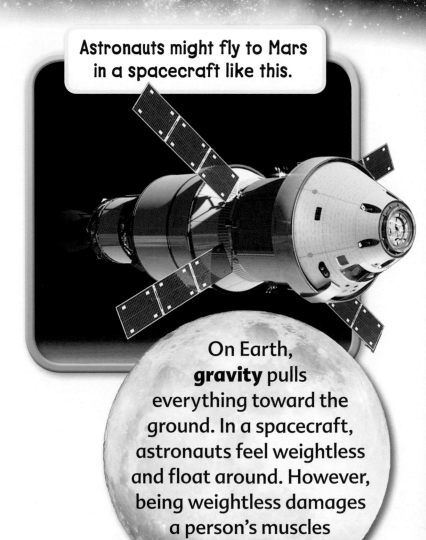

Astronauts might fly to Mars in a spacecraft like this.

On Earth, **gravity** pulls everything toward the ground. In a spacecraft, astronauts feel weightless and float around. However, being weightless damages a person's muscles and bones.

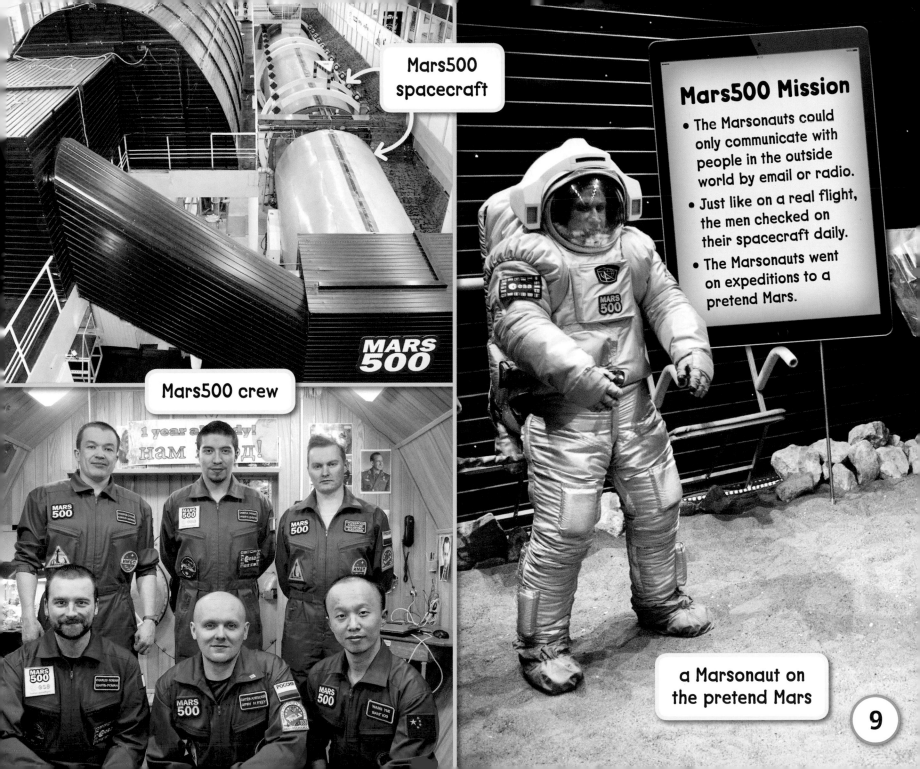

Mars500 spacecraft

Mars500 crew

Mars500 Mission

- The Marsonauts could only communicate with people in the outside world by email or radio.
- Just like on a real flight, the men checked on their spacecraft daily.
- The Marsonauts went on expeditions to a pretend Mars.

a Marsonaut on the pretend Mars

Extreme Planet

If people ever reach Mars, they will find a harsh planet.

The air there contains hardly any **oxygen**, which humans need to breathe.

Mars's air is mostly made up of **carbon dioxide**.

The planet is also freezing cold because it is farther from the Sun than Earth.

Marsonauts will need warm spacesuits that supply them with oxygen.

a distant Sun shining on Mars

The Sun produces **radiation** that can cause cancer and other diseases. Around Earth, a covering called the magnetosphere (mag-NEE-tuh-sfeer) blocks out radiation. However, Mars does not have this protection, so harmful radiation reaches the planet's surface.

The temperature on Mars can drop to -190°F (-123°C)!

an image showing what Marsonauts wearing protective spacesuits might look like

Survival Essentials

To survive on Mars, humans will need water, oxygen, and energy.

Robots could be used to search for ice, which could then be melted to make liquid water.

Water is made up of the gases hydrogen and oxygen.

Special machines can remove oxygen from water.

Then the oxygen could be pumped into habitats and spacesuits.

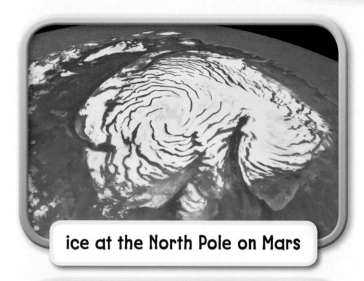

ice at the North Pole on Mars

This illustration shows a large machine collecting ice on Mars.

Solar panels could be set up to make electricity using energy from the Sun. Some of the gases in the air on Mars could be used to make fuel for vehicles.

solar panels

a possible design for a Mars vehicle

13

Home Sweet Home

A home on Mars must protect people from radiation and the cold.

However, getting building materials to Mars will be difficult.

One idea is to build inflatable habitats on Earth that can be shipped to Mars.

Then, instead of air, the shell of the habitat will be filled with ice.

The ice will make a strong home that also keeps out radiation!

a large, underground cave on Earth

Scientists think there are vast underground caves on Mars where people could build homes. Living underground is a good way to keep warm and stay safe from radiation and powerful storms.

Space Farmers

How will the Marsonauts get food?

It would be very hard and expensive to send food from Earth.

So seeds and special greenhouses will be sent to Mars.

Then, the settlers can grow vegetables and fruit—just like farmers on Earth!

Astronauts on the International Space Station (ISS) have successfully grown vegetables in space.

cabbage growing on the ISS

The greenhouse will protect the plants from radiation and keep them warm.

What might a Marsonaut eat in a day? Make a menu for one day. Remember, every food item must be something that can be grown.

Road Trip!

What will Marsonauts do when they're not hard at work?

They might take a road trip in a rover vehicle to visit Mars's Olympus Mons.

This giant volcano is 14 miles (22 km) high!

Or perhaps they will go to Valles Marineris.

This gigantic valley is three times as deep as the Grand Canyon!

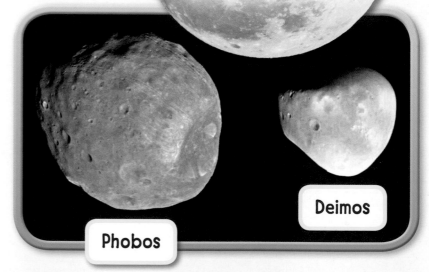

If you were standing on Mars, it's possible to see the planet's two moons—Phobos (FOH-bohss) and Deimos (DEE-mohss).

Phobos

Deimos

If you were on Mars and asked someone a question on Earth, it could take up to 22 minutes to get an answer. Why?

(The answer is on page 24.)

Olympus Mons
(oh-LIM-pus MAHNS)

Valles Marineris
(VAL-iss mare-ih-NARE-us)

19

The First Martians

If living on Mars will be so challenging, why are scientists exploring the idea?

Perhaps someday, Earth will no longer be a safe place to live.

Then, Mars could become a new home for humans.

So who will be the first Martian?

It could be you!

This is a view of space from Mars. What do you think the tiny bright dot could be?

(The answer is on page 24.)

In the future, Mars could become a rest stop for astronauts traveling to more distant places!

21

Science Lab

Design and Build a Mars Habitat!

Design and build a model of a home where people can live on Mars.

You will need:
- Paper and colored pencils or paints
- Scissors
- Glue or tape
- Empty boxes, plastic bottles, toilet paper tubes, or other materials

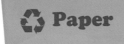

Paper

1. Look at the materials you've collected and think of a design for your habitat.

2. Draw a picture of your design and label its parts.

3. Build a model of your habitat.

Be a Scientist

Write a short report about your habitat, and answer the following questions:

- *What will the outside of your habitat be made of?*

- *Will there be a section for growing food or parking a vehicle?*

- *How many rooms will be inside the habitat, and what will they be used for?*

Science Words

carbon dioxide (KAR-buhn dye-OK-side) a colorless gas that's poisonous to humans in large quantities

gravity (GRA-vuh-tee) the force that causes objects to be pulled toward other objects

habitat (HAB-uh-tat) a special home made for living in an extreme place

oxygen (OK-suh-juhn) a colorless gas in the air that humans need to breathe

poles (POHLZ) the farthest points north and south on a planet

radiation (ray-dee-AY-shuhn) an invisible form of energy that travels in waves

Index

Read More

Bellisario, Gina. *To Mars! (Space Adventures).* Minneapolis, MN: Millbrook (2017).

Markovics, Joyce. *Mars: Red Rocks and Dust (Out of This World).* New York: Bearport (2015).

Owen, Ruth. *Living on Mars (It's A Fact: Real-Life Reads).* New York: Ruby Tuesday (2014).

Learn More Online

To learn more about living on Mars, visit
www.bearportpublishing.com/space-ology

About the Author

Ellen Lawrence lives in the United Kingdom and fully admits to being a huge space geek! While researching and writing this series, she loved watching interviews with astronauts and spine-tingling launch countdowns.

Answers

Page 18: It can take up to 22 minutes for a signal from a radio or computer to travel from Mars to Earth because the two planets are so far apart.

Page 20: The tiny bright dot is Earth.